Wet and Dry

By Emily C. Dawson

RiverStream Readers
Great Reading • Real Learning

Learn to Read	**Read Independently**	**Read to Know More**
Frequent repetition of sentence structures, high frequency words, and familiar topics provide ample support for brand new readers. Approximately 100 words.	Repetition is mixed with varied sentence structures and 6 to 8 content words per book are introduced with photo labels and picture glossary supports. Approximately 150 words.	These books feature a higher text load with additional nonfiction features such as more photos, timelines, and text divided into sections. Approximately 250 words.

Accelerated Reader methodology uses Level A instead of Pre 1. We have chosen to change it for ease of understanding by potential users.

Amicus Readers hardcover editions published by Amicus. P.O. Box 1329, Mankato, Minnesota 56002 www.amicuspublishing.us

Series Editor — Rebecca Glaser
Series Designer — Christine Vanderbeek
Photo Researcher — Heather Dreisbach

RiverStream Publishing reprinted by arrangement with Appleseed Editions Ltd.

Library of Congress Cataloging-in-Publication Data
Dawson, Emily C.
Wet and dry places / by Emily C. Dawson.
p. cm. — (Amicus Readers. Let's compare)
Includes index.
Summary: "Compares and contrasts wet and dry places around the world, such as rain forests and deserts. Includes comprehension activity"—Provided by publisher.
ISBN 978-1-60753-004-6 (library binding)
1. Deserts—Juvenile literature. 2. Rain forests–Juvenile literature. 3. Deserts. 4. Rain forests. I. Title.
QH88.R87 2012
577—dc22
2010041755

Photo Credits
Getty Images/Wilfried Krecichwost, Cover top, 8, 21m, 22ml; MICHAEL FAY/National Geographic Stock, Cover bottom, 12; Morley Read/iStockphoto, 4, 21t, 22mr; Digital Vision, 6; STEVE RAYMER/National Geographic Stock, 10; Holger Mette/iStockphoto, 14, 21b, 22bl; DINODIA PICTURE AGENCY /Getty Images/© Oxford Scientific , 16t, 20b; Danita Delimont/Getty Images, 16b, 22br; TED MEAD/photolibrary, 18t, 20m, 22tl; KEN STEPNELL/photolibrary, 18b; Pgiam/iStockphoto, 20t, 22tr

1 2 3 4 5 CG 15 14 13 12
RiverStream Publishing—Corporate Graphics, Mankato, MN—112012—1002CGF12

Table of Contents

4

Let's compare wet and dry places.

The Amazon rain forest is a wet place. Rainwater forms waterfalls there.

Deserts are dry.

It hardly ever rains.

Sounds are wet.

A sound is a place

where the ocean goes

between mountains.

Some mountains get a lot of rain. One mountain in Hawaii gets rain for 300 days of the year.

Deserts can be windy. The wind makes big hills called sand dunes.

14

Tundra is dry. It gets only a little more rain than a desert.

Let's Compare!

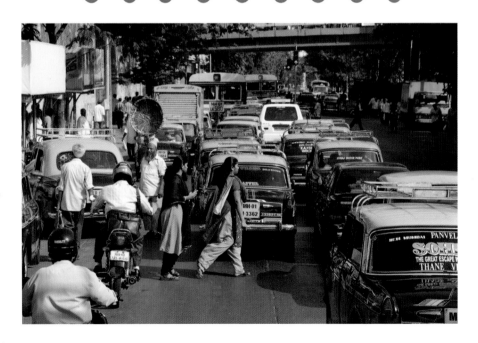

Some places are both wet and dry. Heavy rains called monsoons fall in India. But other times it is dry.

Let's Compare!

Some places flood in the summer. But then winter is dry. Do you live in a wet or dry place?

Let's Compare!
Picture Glossary

desert →
a dry area of land
where few plants grow;
little rain falls in deserts.

← flood
an overflowing of
water from a river

monsoon →
a strong wind that
brings very heavy rain

← rain forest
a tropical forest where a lot of rain falls

sound →
a long, narrow area of water between the mainland and an island

← tundra
a cold area where there are no trees

Wet and Dry Places

Look at the photos.
1. Which places are wet?
2. Which places are dry?
3. Which places can be both?

Ideas for Parents and Teachers

Books 1 through 5 in the RiverStream Readers Level Pre 1 Series give children the opportunity to compare familiar concepts with lots of reading support. Repetitive sentence structures and high frequency words provide appropriate support for new readers. In each book, the picture glossary defines new vocabulary and the "Let's Compare" activity page reinforces compare and contrast techniques.

Before Reading
- Ask the child about the difference between wet and dry places. Ask: Where is a wet place? Where is a dry place?
- Discuss the cover photos. What do these photos tell them?
- Look at the picture glossary together. Read and discuss the words.

Read the Book
- "Walk" through the book and look at the photos. Ask questions or let the child ask questions about the photos.
- Read the book to the child or have him or her read independently.
- Show the child how to refer back to the picture glossary and read the definitions to understand the full meaning.

After Reading
- Have the child identify the wet places and the dry places in the photographs.
- Prompt the child to think more, asking questions such as What do we wear when it rains? What do we wear when it is dry?

Let's Compare!

Index

Web Sites

Biome/Habitat Animal Printouts
www.enchantedlearning.com/biomes

Biomes-Geography for Kids
www.kidsgeo.com/geography-for-kids/0165-biomes.php

Rain & Floods
www.weatherwizkids.com/weather-rain.htm

What's It Like Where You Live?
www.mbgnet.net/sets/